IMAGES
of America

FORT LAWTON

IMAGES
of America

FORT LAWTON

Jack W. Jaunal

ARCADIA
PUBLISHING

Published by Arcadia Publishing
Charleston SC, Chicago IL, Portsmouth NH, San Francisco CA

Printed in the United States of America

Library of Congress Catalog Card Number: 2007939186

For all general information contact Arcadia Publishing at:
Telephone 843-853-2070
Fax 843-853-0044
E-mail sales@arcadiapublishing.com
For customer service and orders:
Toll-Free 1-888-313-2665

Visit us on the Internet at www.arcadiapublishing.com

This early (c. 1900) photograph by civil engineer Ambrose Kiehl shows soldiers of a color guard at what is believed to be the first flagpole erected at Fort Lawton when it was established on Magnolia Bluff in Seattle, Washington. Later the flagpole was relocated near the administration building. (Courtesy of University of Washington Libraries, Special Collection, Negative UW 27384.)

CONTENTS

ACKNOWLEDGMENTS

The publication of this pictorial history of Fort Lawton would not have been possible without the assistance of many individuals, especially librarians and archivists. If I have unknowingly infringed on copyright in the writing of this history, I apologize and hope it is accepted. A conscientious effort has been made to obtain required permission. Some of the material is in public domain. I am grateful to the following individuals and say thank you: Julie Albright, my editor at Arcadia Publishing, who provided advice, guidance, suggestions, and editing; Alan H. Archambault, curator of the Fort Lewis Military Museum, for the loan of a copy of National Archives, Record Group 77, Fort Lawton; Nicolette Bromberg, with the University of Washington Libraries Special Collection, for photographs, including the Ambrose Kiehl Collection; Ronald R. Burke, author of *Troopship*, who provided photographs; Michele Clark, with the Olmsted National Historic Site, for the photograph of John Olmsted; Cathleen Cordova for information about the Army Special Services and their various functions; Ann Frantilla, with the Seattle Municipal Archives, for research and photographs; Mary Hammer, with the Washington State Archives, for finding several photographs of the 146th Artillery Regiment, Washington National Guard; Demon Jones, with the National Archives in Seattle; Susan Karren for negatives of the dedication ceremony of Discovery Park; Jacqueline E. A. Lawson, with the Black Heritage Society of Washington State; Emery V. Lehman II, with the Washington National Guard Museum, who provided unlimited access to the holdings; Carolyn Marr, with the Museum of History and Industry, for research and photograph assistance and advice; Patty McNamee, with the National Archives in Seattle; Elaine Miller, with the Washington Historical Society, for research and photograph assistance; Dominic W. Moreo, author of *Riot at Fort Lawton, 1944*, for photograph assistance; Sarah Nelson, with the National Archives in Seattle; Evelyn B. Poalucci, who at the age of 90 provided very interesting conversations about her World II days at Fort Lawton as well as photographs; Anthony Powell for his photographic assistance; Margaret Riddle, with the Everett Public Library; Lisa Scharenhorst, with the Seattle Public Library; Carmen Scott, with the Des Moines (Washington) Historical Society; and Elizabeth Walsh, with the Seattle Public Library.

INTRODUCTION

On February 9, 1900, the fort constructed on Magnolia Bluff in Seattle, Washington, was dedicated in honor of Maj. Gen. Henry Ware Lawton. Building began in June 1898, and the first units of construction were completed in December 1899, followed in the next year by its dedication.

On July 26, 1901, the first of the army troops arrived, the 32nd Coast Artillery Company, followed in August by the 106th Coast Artillery Company. In 1903, construction work at Fort Lawton was ordered to stop. No gun batteries were installed, and within a few years, the civic leaders in Seattle had become disenchanted by the army's failure to develop the fort.

Rather than being rewarded for all their efforts by a major military installation, with all the economic consequences of such an installation, the citizens of Seattle found less than 400 soldiers stationed at the fort by 1908. Although intended primarily as an infantry post, the first soldiers to arrive were artillerymen. The first detachment of infantry assigned to the post was Company B of the 17th Infantry Regiment, arriving on May 3, 1902. Throughout most of its years, Fort Lawton remained an infantry post, especially the early years with two to four companies of infantry. Seattle's hopes for a major military installation were not to be realized.

Shortly before World War I, Camp Lewis, later designated a fort, was established on a large tract of land south of Tacoma, and the army's emphasis on Fort Lawton decreased. At the same time, Seattle's interest in the fort property as a park increased. Fort Lawton remained small in size and influence during the years between World War I and World War II.

Some troop movement and training occurred at Fort Lawton during World War I, and local units of the National Guard and Army Reserve trained there during this period. The Seattle general strike of 1919 caused the stationing of troops in Seattle, and one battalion of infantry was placed in reserve at Fort Lawton.

Seattle's first opportunity to acquire Fort Lawton came in 1938 when the army offered the site to the City of Seattle for $1. Incredibly, the city declined the offer, believing it could not assume the expense of maintaining the area as a park during that period of economic depression.

During World War II, Fort Lawton for the first time became a very active base for the induction, training, embarkation, and debarkation of troops. It was the sixth-largest point of embarkation for troops during the war, the second-largest point of embarkation on the West Coast, and the fourth largest in employment of civilian workers and cargo tonnage. Fort Lawton processed about 793,000 troops for embarkation, about 618,000 troops for debarkation, and 5,000 Italian prisoners of war for transport to Hawaii. When the war ended, 1,150 German prisoners of war were confined at the fort.

The most dramatic event at Fort Lawton during World War II occurred on August 14, 1945, when a former Italian prisoner of war, Guglielmo Olivotto, was hanged. After a fight in the Italian work unit's barracks between African American soldiers and Italian prisoners, the body of Olivotto was later found hanging from a tree.

The largest court-martial of World War II grew out of the investigation following the incident. Forty-one soldiers were charged with rioting, and three were charged with, and found guilty of, murdering Olivotto. The trial judge advocate was Lt. Col. Leon Jaworski and the defense counsel was Maj. William T. Beeks, both destined for distinguished legal careers.

Olivotto is buried at the Fort Lawton Cemetery, which also holds the body of Albert Marquardt, a German prisoner of war. Both graves are located on the periphery of the cemetery, several feet from each other, and separated from all other graves. Olivotto's grave is marked by a broken Roman column signifying a life cut short. The grave of Marquardt is marked by a government headstone and enclosed by a small, white painted wood fence about 1 foot high.

There are two versions about the death of Marquardt, a soldier of the Afrika Korps. One version is he died "accidental" of drinking lacquer thinner, and the second version is he committed suicide because he did not want to return to Germany.

After the conclusion of World War II, Fort Lawton operated as a personnel center, processing the military, their dependants, and Department of Defense civilian employees going to and returning from overseas, with the additional task of separating and assigning army personnel. For a brief period of time during the war in Korea, from 1950 to 1953, the fort became a very active point in the embarkation and debarkation of army troops. In one week, approximately 18,000 soldiers were processed at the fort upon their return from Korea. After the Korean War, Fort Lawton once again reverted to peacetime service.

One of Fort Lawton's principal missions in the cold-war years was to provide two sites for the Nike-Hercules Air Defense System. A control center for this system was installed at the fort and manned by the 49th Air Defense Artillery Group. In 1974, as part of the reduction of missile batteries in the United States, the 49th Air Defense Artillery Group was deactivated on May 29.

In 1968, Fort Lawton was designated a sub-installation of Fort Lewis. That same year, the 124th U.S. Army Reserve Command (ARCOM) was activated with its headquarters located on the fort. The major units at the fort were the U.S. Army Garrison, Fort Lawton; and the 124th U.S. Army Reserve Command.

On April 24, 1964, the Secretary of Defense announced that at least 85 percent of Fort Lawton would be declared "surplus" government land. Seattle officials and various interest groups began to compete in an eight-year campaign for all or part of the land. In 1968, Citizens for Fort Lawton Park, a group of local organizations in favor of Fort Lawton for a city park, was formed. The Bureau of Indian Affairs expressed tentative interest in 1969 for some of the surplus lands. In 1970, the United Indians of All Tribes publicly protested at Fort Lawton to regain the surplus land for the Native American community.

The United Indians of All Tribes was successful in winning a lease of a 17-acre tract of land from Seattle, after the city had received most of the surplus lands. The Daybreak Star Arts and Cultural Center was completed in 1976 on the land leased to the Native Americans and is located on the north end of the former fort area.

In October 1970, Sen. Henry M. Jackson introduced in Congress legislation that allowed the transfer of surplus U.S. property, at no cost, to state and local agencies for parks and recreational purposes. Known informally as the "Fort Lawton Bill," the legislation became the legacy of the parks policy of President Nixon's administration. On September 1, 1972, acting on behalf of President Nixon, his daughter Tricia Nixon Cox transferred 391 acres of Fort Lawton to the City of Seattle.

Another 127 acres were given to Seattle on April 16, 1979. This last parcel of land consisted of the hilltop area that had been retained by the army when most of the land for what became Seattle's Discover Park was transferred in 1972. This portion of the park now contains the park's Fort Lawton Historic District. The historic district was listed on the National Register of Historic Places in August 1978.

Most of the former army buildings have been demolished as part of the City of Seattle's master plan for the park. A few buildings have been retained for park purposes. These buildings are an important link with the history of Seattle, the state, and the nation. The buildings are noteworthy because they represent a period of time in which military installations like Fort Lawton had a significant role in the social and recreational lives of many communities from the turn of the century until after World War II.

Fort Lawton was founded as a consequence of the first comprehensive study of national defense. The Puget Sound region was virtually without a garrison of troops. At precisely that moment in history, the City of Seattle sought a military installation to revitalize its depressed economy. Had the time not been militarily and economically right, Seattle's efforts to have a fort on Magnolia Bluff might never have met with success. When Fort Lewis was established south of Tacoma, Fort Lawton lost any importance it may have had and never became a major army installation. The return of its land to the people of Seattle completes a series of events that shaped its historic past.

One

THE BEGINNING YEARS

War Department General Order 20, dated February 9, 1900, designated the new army post on Magnolia Bluff Fort Lawton in honor of Maj. Henry Ware Lawton, who was awarded the Medal of Honor during the Civil War. Lawton was commissioned from the enlisted ranks and served as a lieutenant in the 41st Infantry. During the Indian Wars, he served as a captain under the command of Gen. Nelson Miles. His relentless pursuit of the Native American leader Geronimo through Arizona and Mexico was the primary reason Geronimo surrendered to Miles in 1886. Lawton was promoted to major general during the Spanish-American War and his troops captured Siboney and El Caney, Cuba. Transferred to the Philippines, Lawton served under the command of Maj. Gen. Elwell S. Otis during the Philippine Insurrection. Lawton was killed at the Battle of San Mateo on December 19, 1898. The leader of the Filipino troops was, reportedly, named "Geronimo." (Courtesy of National Archives, 111-SC-83947.)

In 1881, the federal government, to meet maritime needs, constructed the West Point Lighthouse and two residences on the promontory, ending in an elongated sand spit from the base of Magnolia Bluff. The first lighting systems were lamps fueled by fish or whale oil and later kerosene. The lenses were manufactured by L. Sautier, Lemonnier et Cie a Paris, at an unknown date. A hand crank activated the foghorns. The West Point Lighthouse was automated in 1985, the last in Washington State to be converted. (Courtesy of National Archives Records Center, Seattle.)

Looking at the base of Magnolia Bluff west from Fort Lawton, the West Point sand spit extends some 600 yards into Puget Sound. The Native American name for the point is Pak'dz Eluc, or "to thrust far out." It refers to the way the point seems to thrust forward into Puget Sound. (Courtesy of National Archives Records Center, Seattle.)

Magnolia Bluff was named by Lt. George Davidson during a U.S. Coast Survey in 1857, mistakenly identifying red-barked madrona trees as magnolias. The nearly vertical cliffs, 250 to 350 feet above sea level, expose a record of the Ice Age and an archaeological history of 25,000 years. (Courtesy of University of Washington Libraries, Special Collection, UW 27385.)

By the end of November 1896, Ambrose Kiehl, a civil engineer under the direction of army quartermaster Capt. W. W. Robinson Jr., provided a detailed topographical map of the proposed site for a military post on Magnolia Bluff. The summit of the Magnolia Bluff plateau is 375 feet above sea level. In the distance is the West Point Lighthouse. (Courtesy of University of Washington Libraries, Special Collection, SEA2033.)

Brig. Gen. Nelson A. Miles, commander of the Columbia Department, in 1885 informed his superiors for the need of fortifications to protect Puget Sound. Later, in 1889, Miles, the general-in-chief of the army (1895–1903), declared there were enough forts around Puget Sound and there was "no necessity" for another "at the present time." Miles is noted in the military history of the Pacific Northwest as the army officer to whom the American Indian leader Chief Joseph of the Nez Perce surrendered in 1877. Nine years later, on September 4, 1886, the Apache Indian leader Geronimo also surrendered to Miles. (Courtesy of Library of Congress, LC-DIG-cwpb-06150.)

General Elwell S. Otis

Brig. Gen. Ewell S. Otis, commander of the Columbia Department, in 1895 explained the advantages of Magnolia Bluff as a point from which a proper system of defenses for Puget Sound could be developed. Originally it was to be a base or headquarters for a coastal artillery system. Stationing a garrison of troops there, not more than a regiment or less than four companies of artillery, would be the "initial act." Otis and Miles served under the command of Gen. John Pope during the Red River Indian War against the Sioux. Otis commanded the 22nd Infantry, and Miles commanded the 5th Infantry and troops of the 6th Cavalry. (Courtesy of National Archives.)

In 1895, the general-in-chief of the army, Gen. John Schofield, who was bald and magnificently whiskered, strongly favored Magnolia Bluff as a site for the establishment of an army post. Schofield years earlier had also strongly favored Pearl Harbor for the establishment of a military base. Schofield's successor as general-in-chief of the army was General Miles, who had a different view by 1889. Miles's objection was overruled by Secretary of War Daniel Lamont. Miles became the last general-in-chief of the army; in 1903, the position became the chief of staff of the army. (Courtesy of Library of Congress, C-USZ-111947.)

This view of Magnolia Bluff, in the background, and the site of Fort Lawton looks northwest from Beacon Hill in Seattle around 1897. The plan for Fort Lawton was approved by Secretary of War Lamont on February 15, 1988. At this time, all titles to lands for Fort Lawton had been conveyed to the United States. (Courtesy of Library of Congress, Historic American Buildings Survey, "Fort Lawton: A Record.")

In June 1898, loggers began to clear 97 acres of old-growth timber for the site of Fort Lawton on Magnolia Bluff at the outer limits of Seattle. Landowners on Magnolia Bluff had donated over 700 acres to the federal government for a new army post. The estimated cost to clear timber and preparation of the ground for building was, in July 1898, about $300 per acre. (Courtesy of Library of Congress, Historic American Buildings Survey, "Fort Lawton: A Record.")

Land clearing consisted of the removal of all trees (except designated shade trees), all brush, logs, rocks, and other rubbish of worthless material, including stumps and roots to a depth of 18 inches. All harvested timber was removed from the property and all refuse was buried on the ground within post boundaries. (Courtesy of Library of Congress, Historic American Buildings Survey, "Fort Lawton: A Record.")

The house for civil engineer Ambrose Kiehl and his family was located near the hospital at the northeast corner of the original clearing. Around 1900, it was moved to the non-commissioned officers' quarters area and was later demolished. Later, around 1905, the Kiehl family moved to Queen Ann Hill in Seattle. (Courtesy of Library of Congress, Historic American Buildings Survey, "Fort Lawton: A Record.")

The family of Ambrose Kiehl is seen here on the front porch of their home in the first officers' quarters. The Kiehl daughters, Laura and Lorena, are on each side of their mother. The first officers' quarters were completed in December 1899. All were of wood construction with Chuckanut stone 20 inches thick and lined in brick foundations. The houses are characteristic of that period of time and have an architectural style of their own. (Courtesy of Library of Congress, Historic American Buildings Survey, "Fort Lawton: A Record.")

Officers' quarters had steam heat, oil lights, water, and sewer connections. Electric lights were installed in 1905, as were water meters in 1913. On January 25, 1889, a Seattle ordinance authorized a water main to Fort Lawton. It was the first system to run outside the city limits to supply water to a distant point. New maple floors were installed in the quarters in 1937. (Courtesy of University of Washington Libraries, Special Collection, Negative UW 27403.)

Double officers' quarters were completed on March 3, 1905, at a cost of $8,715. Water meters were installed on March 7, 1913, at a cost of $10. Seattle water was 8¢ per thousand gallons, although the original agreement with Fort Lawton was to be 3¢ per thousand gallons. (Courtesy of University of Washington Libraries, Special Collection, Negative 27405.)

At Fort Lawton, quarters or barracks for the bachelor officers' quarters (BOQ) were not constructed at Lawton in the early years. The interior finishes of all officers' quarters included plaster on lath walls, hardwood floors, and pressed-metal ceilings. (Courtesy of University of Washington Libraries, Special Collection, Negative UW 27401.)

Field-grade single officers' quarters were completed on March 31, 1904, at a cost of $12,411. Water and sewer connections and electric lights were installed. It had a total floor space of 3,700 square feet. The first field-grade officers to use these quarters were colonels. (Courtesy of National Archives, Record Group 77.)

Double non-commissioned officers' (NCOs) quarters were completed on December 30, 1899, at a cost of $1,688. Married NCO housing was scarce and located near the warehouses and away from the officers' quarters. The first married NCO housing was for "staff" and not "line" NCOs. (Courtesy of National Archives, Record Group 77.)

Livestock next to the officers' quarters in the winter of 1899–1900 was later relocated, probably for olfactory reasons, to Fort Lawton's north area. (Courtesy of Library of Congress, Historic American Buildings Survey, "Fort Lawton: A Record.")

Originally the hospital and stables were to have been at the south of the parade grounds; however, the hospital was built instead at the north end. The change of site was on the recommendation of Quartermaster Capt. W. W. Robinson Jr. because "such a location is near the business end of the post site, at a suitable and convenient distance from the administration building, and sufficiently remote from the officers' quarters, so as not to be objectionable." (Courtesy of Library of Congress, Historic American Buildings Survey, "Fort Lawton: A Record.")

The hospital was completed on February 21, 1900, at a cost of $20,500. It was of wood construction with a stone and brick foundation, a slate roof, and wood and cement floors. There was a bed capacity for 40 patients. Electric lights were installed in 1905; prior lighting was by mineral oil. The steward's quarters (left) was later moved to the enlisted quarters area. During World War II, bed space was increased from 40 to 150 beds. (Courtesy of National Archives and Records Center, Seattle.)

The first double barracks at the edge of the cleared parade ground were completed in December 1899 at a cost of $17,374.06. Steam heating was installed and mineral oil was used for lighting. Electric lights were installed in 1909. There were six bathtubs and, in 1928, four enclosed showers. (Courtesy of National Archives and Records Center, Seattle.)

This 1904 view across from the parade ground shows double four-company barracks, the post-exchange (PX), band barrack, and guardhouse. As with all coastal installations, the Lawton buildings were constructed of wood. Most army posts inland from the coast were constructed of brick and masonry. (Courtesy of National Archives and Records Center, Seattle.)

A view across from the parade ground in 1981 reveals double four-company barracks that were no longer occupied and later demolished. The buildings were typical of that period and were grouped around the parade ground, traditionally the center of army garrisons. (Author's collection.)

The enlisted barracks were doubled to four-company capacity in 1904. The barracks were frame with stone and brick foundations. Coal was used for hot water and heat until 1908, after which steam was used. There were 6 toilets, 4 urinals, 2 wash sinks, and 14 washbasins for 100 soldiers. After March 1, 1916, one hundred wood lockers were installed. Four showers were installed in 1928. (Courtesy of University of Washington Libraries, Special Collection, Negative UKW 27404.)

In 1904, Fort Lawton underwent a second major building phase. The number of officers' quarters increased to a total of 16. By 1909, there were streetlights along Washington Avenue in front of the quarters and a water tower in place. It became the norm in the 20th century for the officers' quarters to be a more exclusive area and the enlisted quarters and barracks located some distance away from "Officers' Country," also known as "Officers' Row" at Fort Lawton. (Courtesy of National Archives and Records Center, Seattle.)

The guardhouse was completed April 24, 1902, and consisted of two steel cages and three cells. The solitary confinement cells were off from the main guardroom. The guardhouse was located near the enlisted barracks, and enlisted soldiers primarily performed the duty of the guard. (Courtesy of National Archives, Record Group 77.)

The storehouse was completed October 22, 1899, at a cost of $3,702. It later became a commissary. Warehouses, shops, and stables were located at an angle from the enlisted quarters. (Courtesy of National Archives, Record Group 77.)

While Fort Lawton was under construction in 1900, the 1st Cavalry Regiment camped in some of the cleared area. Seventy-two years later, an army reserve center at Lawton would be named in honor of a 1st Cavalry soldier, Robert R. Leisy. (Courtesy of University of Washington Libraries, Special Collections, Negative UW 27399.)

These are soldiers of the 1st Cavalry Regiment at Fort Lawton around 1900. The 1st Cavalry Regiment was originally organized as the U.S. Regiment of Dragoons on March 4, 1883. It was re-designated as the 1st Regiment of Dragoons in 1836 and on August 3, 1861, became the 1st Cavalry Regiment. (Courtesy of University of Washington Libraries, Special Collections, Negative UW 27400.)

These are soldiers at muster or troop formation, probably of the 1st Cavalry Regiment, around 1900. The 1st Cavalry Regiment arrived at Fort Lawton from Fort Yellowstone, Wyoming, in 1899. (Courtesy of University of Washington Libraries, Special Collection, Negative UW 27402.)

One of Fort Lawton's main functions in the future became evident in August 1900 when it began to transit soldiers, "casuals," for duty in Alaska and the Philippines. Fort Lawton became a port of embarkation and debarkation from the date it was completed. The U.S. Army Transport (USAT) *Lawton* was among several ships that transported troops to China during the Boxer Rebellion and the Philippine Insurrection. (Courtesy of University of Washington Libraries, Special Collections, Negative UW 27389.)

Cavalrymen of Troop C, 9th Cavalry Regiment, pose in front of their tents at Fort Lawton prior to their embarkation for the Philippines on August 10, 1900. After service in the Philippines, the 9th Cavalry Regiment participated in the 1904 maneuvers at American Lake, Washington. The 9th Cavalry served three tours of duty in the Philippines. (Courtesy of the University of Washington Libraries, Special Collection, Negative Peiser 10095.)

Soldiers of Company A, 7th Infantry Regiment, are seen here in formation prior to their embarkation in 1900 for the Philippine Islands. The 7th Infantry served on Samar in the Philippines from 1901 to 1902. (Courtesy of the University of Washington Libraries, Special Collection, Negative UW 256974.)

The stables and corrals were at first located on the south end of Fort Lawton where the horses and mules would be close to the supply of feed. Later they were moved to the northwest end to be with the warehouses and shops. In 1908, new corrals were constructed to contain 500 horses and mules periodically collected for shipment to the Philippines. Also, several shops, storehouses, offices, and a veterinary hospital were added. (Courtesy of University of Washington Libraries, Special Collection, Negative 27388.)

Many former bunkhouses for civilian horse handlers were changed to quarters for married enlisted soldiers in 1908. The average cost of the housing was $136, and each had coal heat, electric lights, water, and sewer connections. Some had four small rooms on the second (attic) floor. (Courtesy of National Archives, Record Group 77.)

Col. John H. Wholley, for whom Camp Wholley at Fort Lawton was named, commanded the 1st Washington Volunteer Infantry Regiment during the Spanish-American War. Wholley was a graduate of the Military Academy at West Point, New York, and when selected to command the volunteers, he was military instructor of military science, civil engineering, and mathematics at the University of Washington. During its service in the Philippines, from October 1898 to July 1899, the regiment served in three expeditions under the command of Gen. Henry Ware Lawton. After visiting in Seattle with veterans of the Washington Volunteers, Wholley died on January 12, 1914, while traveling to his next assignment at the University of California. (Courtesy of Washington State Archives, Military Collection.)

Seen here are troops in formation during an annual military training encampment of school cadets (left) and soldiers, commonly referred to as Camp Wholley. The camp was named after Col. John H. Wholley, a veteran of the Philippine campaign and a professor of military science, civil engineering, and mathematics at the University of Washington. (Courtesy of University of Washington Libraries, Special Collection, Negative UW 27398.)

Soldiers of the 10th Infantry Regiment relieved those of the 19th Infantry Regiment in 1905. The 19th served at Panay and Cebu in the Philippines during the Philippine Insurrection. The 10th Infantry Regiment served in the Philippines from 1899 to 1901. The regiment consisted of approximately 22 officers and 333 enlisted soldiers while stationed at Fort Lawton. The officer on the right is armed with the sword as prescribed by Fort Lawton General Order 17, paragraph II, "The sword will be worn by Officers upon all occasions of duty under arms, tactical drills and target practice." (Courtesy University of Washington Libraries, Special Collection, Negative UW 14734.)

Soldiers of the 32nd Coast Artillery Company and the 106th Artillery Company were stationed at Fort Lawton from 1901 to the summer of 1902. In May, the 32nd Artillery was sent to Fort Liscum, Alaska, and the 106th was ordered to Skagway. On May 9, 1902, Company B, 17th Infantry Regiment, arrived. Like other regiments assigned to Fort Lawton, the 17th had served in the Philippines from 1899 to 1900. The 19th Infantry Regiment arrived at Lawton in 1903 and the 17th Infantry Regiment departed. Soldiers in front of the post PX around 1905 are probably from the 19th Infantry. The band barracks and guardhouse are the other buildings. (Courtesy University of Washington Libraries, Special Collection, Curtis 14735.)

Soldiers from the Military Police Battalion stand in front of the PX in 1974. Trees are higher, the guardhouse is hidden from view, and street lighting along a paved Oregon Avenue and some of the buildings on the hill to the right are out of view. (Frederick Mann photograph, courtesy of Library of Congress, Historic American Buildings Survey, "Fort Lawton: A Record.")

Sometime in the early 1900s, a saluting cannon was placed in front of Officers' Row. It was relocated in 1924 to the main entrance of the fort and in 1956 moved to another area. It was last located in the quadrangle of the Army Reserve Leisy Center. (University of Washington Libraries, Special Collection, Negative UW 4792.)

During a visit to Seattle on May 24, 1903, Pres. Theodore Roosevelt went for a horseback ride at Fort Lawton with two companions and later toured the area and watched soldiers play a game of baseball. At this time, 108 soldiers of the 19th Infantry Regiment, 19 soldiers of the 8th Infantry Regiment, 15 soldiers of the 13th Infantry Regiment, 2 soldiers of the Coast Artillery, 3 soldiers of the Signal Corps, and 1 soldier from the 23rd Infantry Regiment were garrisoned at Fort Lawton. (Courtesy Library of Congress, LC-USZ-131913.)

Soldiers watch a baseball game when not on duty, probably on a Saturday or Sunday. In the distance is Camp Wholley, with the tents located between the enlisted barracks and the PX. The same space was later used as a tent bivouac by the army from 1906 to 1909 and again in the early years of World War II. The camp was name after Col. John H. Wholley, who served as the commanding officer of the 1st Washington Volunteer Infantry Regiment in the Philippines during the 1899 insurrection. (Courtesy of Library of Congress, Historic American Buildings Survey, "Fort Lawton: A Record.")

The normal routine at this time was often repeated to keep the soldiers busy. Equipment, personal and government, needed maintenance and cleaning. The parade ground needed mowing, and around the barracks needed policing. Many hours were spent at drill and marksmanship training. Saturday mornings were for troop inspection by the commanding officers. Tuesdays and Sundays, the band gave a concert. Saturday and Sunday afternoons, there were often baseball games between various companies or units. A soldier's pay was $13 per month, and some NCOs were paid $18 per month. (Courtesy of National Archives, 319-Law-6.)

Fort Lawton General Order 17, dated December 10, 1901, stated, "Officers and enlisted men will wear the blue undress uniform and forage cap on the reservation. . . . The campaign hat will be worn with the blue undress uniform by non-commissioned officers in charge of fatigue parties, by the prison guard, at target practice, with leggings and during rainy weather. White gloves will be worn on all occasions of ceremony and duty, except on fatigue and the rubber clothing is worn. Enlisted men will not appear out of barracks without being properly dressed. The uniform will invariably be buttoned throughout. Enlisted men will invariably salute Officers wherever they may be. The khaki uniform will be worn only when authorized by the Post Commander. All company officers will attend the drills and other exercises prescribed for their organizations unless specially excused by the Post Commander. The officer of the day will attend reveille and retreat roll calls. All enlisted men of the companies will be required to answer to their names at these roll calls except the cooks, the sick in the hospital and such men as are authorized to be absent by the Post Commander." (Courtesy of National Archives, 319-Law-7.)

Soldiers of the Washington National Guard 2nd Infantry Regiment and National Guard Coast Artillery Corps participated in team and individual rifle matches at Fort Lawton in 1911 and 1912. Participants complained about insufficient accommodations and unsatisfactory rifle-range conditions. Prior to having their own rifle range, soldiers from Fort Lawton went to American Lake, one company at a time, for rifle practice. (Courtesy of Washington State Historical Society, Tacoma, Military Collection.)

The original 300-yard rifle range at Fort Lawton was considered inadequate and was extended at times but never to the 3,000 yards desired. In 1910, Maj. Hiram Chittenden of the Army Engineer Corps recommended that a new rifle range be installed in the tidal flats below Magnolia Bluff, but the recommendation was not acted on. (Courtesy of National Archives, Seattle.)

Fort Lawton was open to the public, and visitors could observe dress parades and guard mounts three days a week, listen to concerts by the army band on Tuesdays and Sundays, and take in an occasional "Trooping of the Colors." (Courtesy of Museum of History and Industry, Seattle, 2002.48.836.)

Soldiers of the 25th Infantry Regiment arrived at Fort Lawton on October 5, 1909, after their service in the Philippines. The 1st Battalion, the Regimental Headquarters, and the regimental band remained; the 2nd and 3rd Battalions were sent to Fort Wright near Spokane. Some of the assignments for the 2nd and 3rd Battalions were to fight forest fires in the national forests and to help local police when workers of the IWW (Industrial Workers of the World) went on strike. The 25th Infantry bandleader was Leslie V. King (far left), who was among the first "colored bandmasters" of the "all colored regiments," according to an Anthony Powell article in the summer 2007 edition of *Army History Magazine*. Among the NCO wives at Lawton was Rafina Clemente Jenkins, who with her five children immigrated to the United States to be with her husband, Sgt. Francis Jenkins. She was the first Filipina in Washington State. The 25th Regiment left Fort Lawton on January 1, 1912. (Courtesy of the private collection of Anthony Powell.)

COPYRIGHT 1908
BY G. V. BUCK.

When two petitions signed by community residents near Fort Lawton requested the withdrawal of the 25th Regiment, Pres. William H. Taft stated, "It was very clear that the request cannot be complied with." These were "United States troops" and they would be "stationed and housed in the United States." Taft's attitude in regards to the African American population is noted in his inaugural address as president: "Their ancestors came here years ago against their wish, and this is their only country and only flag. They have shown themselves anxious to live for it and die for it. Encountering the race feelings against them, subject at times to cruel injustice growing out of it, they may well have our profound sympathy and aid in the struggle they are making." (Courtesy of Library of Congress, LC-USZ-48758.)

To encourage the establishment of Fort Lawton on Magnolia Bluff, the West Street and North End Electric Railway Company promised to extend its service to the new post and charge only a 10¢ fare to and from Seattle. By 1900, Stone and Webster, a national utility cartel, had bought up most of Seattle's separate streetcar companies and was granted a 40-year franchise to operate the city's system. The city mandated a 5¢ fare. The "trolley" ran on an hourly and half-hourly schedule throughout the day. In 1909, trolley cars could travel on Fort Lawton to a station building about 200 yards from the administration building. The Seattle Electric Company published the small guide "Trolley Trips about Seattle: Where to Go and How to Get There." Streets that followed the trolley tracks at this time were completely navigable by carriage or automobile. (Courtesy of Washington State Historical Society, Tacoma, Fort-Law 2.)

In 1910, the Seattle Parks Commission requested John Olmsted investigate the possibilities of improvements at Fort Lawton as part of a plan for city parks and parkways. Olmsted's report suggested a number of improvements that he believed would better serve the army and at the same time permit the development of roadways, open spaces, and access for Seattle residents to enjoy certain areas of the fort. (Courtesy of National Park Service, Frederick Law Olmsted National Historic Site, JOB2931.)

Although the Olmsted plan was forwarded by army officials to the Secretary of War, no action was taken. Subsequent clearing of forest and roadway construction at Lawton were generally consistent with the ideas of civil engineer Kiehl and army captain W. W. Robinson. (Courtesy of Seattle Department of Parks and Recreation.)

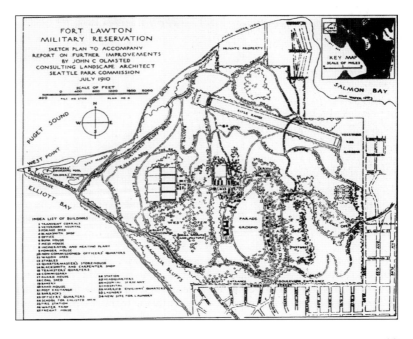

Col. Hiram M. Chittenden, who took command of the U.S. Army Corps of Engineers in Seattle in 1906, was brought into the Seattle city sewer project for consultation as the local army engineer. At the time, Chittenden was supervising the building of his docks linking Puget Sound and Salmon Bay at Ballard. The government locks linking Puget Sound and Salmon Bay at Ballard are named after him. Chittenden believed that Lawton, "from a scenic point of view," was "one of the most beautiful and park-like reservations now belonging to the government." (Courtesy of University of Washington Libraries, Special Collection, UW 2762.)

In 1910, the City of Seattle proposed a sewer system to be built under Fort Lawton to an outfall on the north shore. When completed in 1913, the North Trunk System, a 12-foot-diameter brick-lined tunnel and a 48-inch outfall, carried sewage to the beach at West Point. The system became the predecessor to the West Point treatment plant. (Courtesy of Seattle Municipal Archives, 5978.)

Raw sewage from homes and businesses was discharged into Puget Sound at West Point, where it was believed that nature would take care of it. Unfortunately, the beach became unsuitable for sea life and unfit for human enjoyment. By the 1950s, an estimated 40 million gallons per day emptied into Puget Sound. (Courtesy of Seattle Municipal Archives, 5980.)

In 1914, Fort Lawson was garrisoned by a four-company battalion of the 14th Infantry Regiment with support elements. It was also the regimental headquarters, and by 1915, it became the headquarters of the 7th Infantry Brigade. At this time, the army was preparing for possible involvement in World War I. In planning for a potential war, army captain Burns and Mrs. Phillips of the Red Cross discuss Red Cross training and other activities in July 1916. (Courtesy of Washington State Historical Society, Tacoma, Port-Bur-10.)

Fort Lawton remained basically an infantry post until several months before World War I, when a coast artillery detachment was stationed there. After World War I, Lawton reverted to an infantry post until 1921, when engineers replaced the infantry. Some movement and training of troops occurred at Lawton during World War I, and local units of the Washington National Guard and Army Reserve trained there during this period. The mounted troops on this day in May 1918 may have been among them. (Courtesy of Museum of History and Industry, Seattle, 83.10.1017.)

The Seattle general strike (February 6–11, 1919) led to the mobilization of federal troops within the city. The 1st Battalion, 1st Infantry Regiment, was sent to Fort Lawton as a reserve, and other detachments were stationed at various locations around the city. Each soldier was issued 120 rounds of ammunition and maintained a state of readiness. The strike was orderly, and the use of troops was not needed. Soldiers of the 44th Infantry Regiment less Company C garrisoned Lawton in 1919. (Courtesy of University of Washington, Special Collection.)

In September 1925, sixty-eight horses of the 146th Field Artillery Regiment of the Washington National Guard were stabled at Fort Lawton. Among them was George, the "dancing horse" photographed with his dance instructor, Dorthea Richmond, dancing the Charleston. The Charleston was a jazz dance craze during the Roaring Twenties. (Courtesy of Museum of History and Industry, Seattle, PEMCO Webster and Stevens Collection.)

The 146th Field Artillery Regiment is on parade in 1925. Horse-drawn caissons are to the right and the regimental band on the left. On April 15, 1931, the horses were exchanged for tractors, and all horses, saddles, harnesses, and other material were returned to the federal government. (Courtesy of Washington State Archives, Olympia, Military Collection.)

The 146th Field Artillery band not only participated in military parades but also gave band concerts for both military and civilian audiences. The bandstand at Fort Lawton, now demolished, was one of the sites where the band performed. (Courtesy of Washington State Historical Society, Tacoma.)

In May 1923, Brig. Gen. Clarence B. Blethen of the Washington National Guard (WNG) presented a marble drinking fountain with marker to Fort Lawton. General Blethen also held a colonel's commission in the U.S. Army Coast Artillery Corps. He was appointed commanding officer of the 1st Coast Defense Command, Coast Artillery Corps, WNG, in 1916 and the Coast Defense of Puget Sound in 1917. In 1923, Blethen commanded the WNG encampment at Camp Murray and in 1924 commanded the 81st Infantry Brigade, WNG. He was promoted to brigadier general, WNG, in 1924. Blethen was the publisher of the *Seattle Times* from 1915 to 1941. In 1977, the C. B. Blethen Memorial Awards were established for newspaper reporting in Washington, Montana, Idaho, Utah, Alaska, and Alberta and British Columbia, Canada. (Courtesy of Washington State Historical Society, Tacoma, 10328.)

The Clarence B. Blethen drinking fountain is located in Freedom Grove, near the chapel and Korea War Memorial, and the marker reads: "Presented by Clarence B. Blethen, Brigadier, General, WNG Late, Colonel, CACUS Army, May 1923." In 1956, the drinking fountain was rededicated after it had been relocated from its original site to Freedom Grove. The Korea War Memorial is in the shadow of the tree in the background. (Author's collection.)

The first junior citizens' military training camp ever held in the United States, named Camp Lawton, was at Fort Lawton on September 4 and 5 in 1925. Some 517 boys between the ages of 12 and 14 attended. Although the encampment was strongly endorsed by many civic leaders and parents, a small group of people protested the "war camp" that "set up" so many "little boys to the infection of war," according to the September 4 and 5, 1925, editions of the *Seattle Post Intelligencer* (Courtesy of Seattle Municipal Archives, Photograph Collection, 31351.)

Each boy brought a blanket, toothbrush, and other personal items for an overnight stay. They slept in army tents and ate army "chow" from army mess kits filled with army food from army field kitchens. Dinner consisted of beef stew with vegetable, bread, cookies, jelly, ice cream, and a cup of cocoa. Taps sounded at 10:00 p.m. Reveille was at 5:00 a.m., which was followed by a morning hike and then a breakfast of cantaloupes, fried potatoes, eggs, bread, and coffee, after which they performed calisthenics. (Courtesy of Seattle Municipal Archives, Photograph Collection, 31350.)

After being formed into companies and assigned tents to sleep, the boys witnessed a presentation of various army weapons climaxed by a demonstration by 3rd Battalion, 4th Infantry Regiment, in an attack on an imaginary enemy position. On their final day, there was a review and parade of the 3rd Battalion and its equipment. In appreciation of their stay, the boys presented the commanding officer at Fort Lawton a silver-trimmed riding crop. (Courtesy of Seattle Municipal Archives, Photograph Collection, 31352.)

Two

THE MIDDLE YEARS

Three companies of the Civilian Conservation Corps (CCC) were formed at Fort Lawton in 1933. On April 11, Company A, 96th Battalion, was formed and two weeks later re-designated the 935th Company, followed by the 948th and 984th Companies. The 935th work camp was located at Salt Water Park in Des Moines, Washington. The CCC provided work for unemployed male citizens between 18 and 25 in reforestation, road construction, prevention of soil erosion, and national park and flood control projects under the direction of army officers. The army was responsible for the organization, control, transportation, medical treatment, and payment of the CCC. However, the CCC was not subject to the Articles of War. (Courtesy of Des Moines Historical Society, Des Moines, Washington, 1-28-OOP-.01.)

During the years of the Great Depression, the federal government provided millions of dollars for equipment modernization and enlargement of Fort Lawton's facilities. The work was part of the Federal Emergency Relief Administration (FERA) public works projects. One of the projects was tree-pruning along the fort's streets in November 1933. (Courtesy of University of Washington Libraries, Special Collection, Negative UW 4791.)

A tree pruning project by workers under the Emergency Relief Act (ERA) removed the branches from the trees along Officers' Row in November 1933. The replanting of trees throughout the fort was done by the Work Projects Administration (WPA) under the ERA. In five years, the WPA spent $292,460 on Fort Lawton projects. (Courtesy of University of Washington Libraries, Special Collection, Negative UW 4790.)

Workers of the ERA sodded and graded the land in back of the PX and gymnasium on January 23, 1934. Behind the buildings on the left is the wall of the handball court. Firewood cutting and stacking was another project by workers of the ERA and WPA. (Courtesy of University of Washington Libraries, Special Collection, Negative UW 9212.)

Many of the projects by the ERA and WPA contributed to Fort Lawton becoming Discovery Park. The wooden bridge built by the ERA workers is an example of the park-like image of Fort Lawton. The land-clearing projects at Lawton provided employment for many men. Both the ERA and WPA funded work projects at Lawton from 1933 to 1941. (Courtesy of University of Washington Libraries, Special Collection, Negative UW 27386.)

The standard sidearm for officers in 1938 was the .45-caliber pistol. It was a seven-round, magazine-fed, semiautomatic, single-action hand weapon. It was standard army issue from 1911 through 1992. The shooter wearing the civilian jacket may have been a reservist. (Author's collection.)

Officers clean weapons during target practice. The officer on the right has his captain's insignia of rank on the shoulder of his shirt as worn at that time; later officer insignia of rank would be placed on the collar of the shirt and the shoulder of the coat. Other officers are wearing the jacket of the blue fatigue or work uniform of the pre–World War II years. (Author's collection.)

The combat experience of World War I provided the army with its first significant exposure to chemical warfare. Chemical-warfare training at Fort Lawton in 1938 included the correct use of the gas mask. Training was based on World War I experience. (Author's collection.)

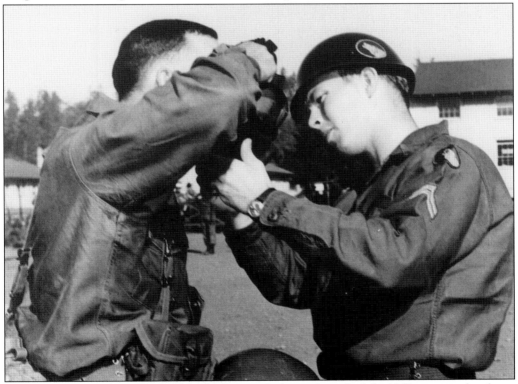

Chemical-warfare training in the use of the gas mask changed very little by 1968—remove headgear, hold one's breath, chin in first, pull straps over head, tighten, cover cylinder, and exhale and inhale to see if the mask is fitted properly and to check for any air leak. The mask must protect the mouth, nose, and eyes and contain features for filtering the incoming air supply. (Author's collection.)

Chemical-warfare training included not only gas but liquid flammable material, thermite, and smoke. Smoke was sometimes used as a ruse for gas and smoke-screen training in 1938. It was the cavalry that brought about the use of smoke in warfare. Because dust clouds created by horses' hooves sometimes helped conceal movement, the use of smoke evolved. (Author's collection.)

Soldiers of the 104th Infantry in 1968 train for riot or crowd control by using smoke as a substitute for the tear gas that would be used in an actual situation. (Author's collection.)

The Daughters of U.S. War Veterans Drill Team of the Fortson-Thygesen Post was actually a drum and trumpet marching group named in honor of Washington National Guard soldiers who sometimes trained at Fort Lawton and died in the Philippines during the Spanish-American War. Capt. George Fortson was killed while on patrol near Pasig. Pvt. Carl Thygesen was killed while on patrol near Morong. (Courtesy of Everett Public Library, Northwest Room, Juleen Studio.)

An aerial view of Fort Lawton in 1934 indicates very little change in landscape since it was established in 1900. The three long wooden-frame buildings in the lower right corner are horse stables. The stables were 30 feet wide and 330 feet long and had a capacity of 192 horses. The cost when completed in 1908 was $3,633. The stables were considered unsuitable on June 6, 1930, and demolished by order of the Secretary of War. (Courtesy of Museum of History and Industry, Webster and Stevens collection, 83.10.17579.1.)

In 1938, the army authorized U.S. congressman (later senator) Warren G. Magnuson to offer Fort Lawton to the City of Seattle for $1. The city council and the mayor, John Dore, declined the offer. Because of the Great Depression, it was considered too expensive to maintain the land as a park. Later, in early 1941, Magnuson informed Seattle city officials that the army had no intention of leaving Fort Lawton. Magnuson was born April 12, 1905, and died May 20, 1989. Except for his navy service during World War II, he served as a U.S. representative from 1939 to 1944 and as a U.S. senator from 1945 to 1980. (Courtesy of Museum of History and Industry, Seattle, SHS 10354.)

This aerial view shows Fort Lawton in 1940 as America was preparing for a possible war. The lower left corner of photograph shows an empty area that was formerly the stables area. It would soon become a barracks area. The small building behind the small white buildings in the lower left corner, in the clear area, was originally the powder magazine. (Courtesy of Museum of History and Industry, Seattle, *Seattle Post-Intelligencer* collection, PI27232.)

In May 1940, it was announced that the army's 149th Interceptor Command Headquarters would be located at Fort Lawton. Because there were not quarters for both the 149th and troops in transit, about 800 soldiers of the 149th lived in tents during the fall and winter of 1941. (Courtesy of Museum of History and Industry, Seattle, *Seattle Post-Intelligencer* collection, PI27235.)

In June 1941, it was announced that because of the unlimited national emergency proclaimed by Pres. Franklin D. Roosevelt, Fort Lawton would receive $920,350 for expansion. Fort Lawton was once again preparing for a possible war. (Courtesy of Museum of History and Industry, Seattle, *Seattle Post-Intelligencer* collection, PI27233.)

The military population at Fort Lawton during World War II was between 15,000 and 20,000 male and female soldiers. Temporary buildings were erected to house them, and some became permanent until after the Korean War. Approximately 370 World War II buildings were demolished prior to the opening of Discovery Park in 1973. (Author's collection.)

The wood-framed barracks had 84,134 square feet of space for the 6 showers, 6 lavatories, 1 urinal, 1 laundry tub, 2 water heaters, 34 windows, and 2 double doors and was heated by a hot-air coal furnace. (Author's collection.)

The wood frame company administration buildings had 17,062 square feet of space and a capacity for 20 personnel. Inside was an office for the company commander, or officer in charge, and the administration area. Heating was provided by a hot-air furnace. (Author's collection.)

This is a wood-frame company storeroom with 12,500 square feet of space that was heated by one coal stove. It held administrative supplies, toilet paper, clean lines for laundry day, foul-weather clothing, and in some an armory. (Author's collection.)

The wood-frame company mess hall was completed on January 19, 1942. It had a capacity to feed 248 soldiers. It had three electric ranges and two refrigerators, two sinks, and coal-heated hot air. Some enlisted mess halls, although identical in appearance, had a smaller capacity of 172 soldiers. (Author's collection.)

The wood-frame company recreation building had 16,625 square feet of space. A few recreation buildings at this time had a piano. Most of the construction was done by WPA workers. (Author's collection.)

The wood-frame post-exchange was completed in 1942. It had 31,588 square feet of space and a coal-fed steam boiler for a heating system. There was one main PX in each of the five troop areas. (Author's collection.)

The wood-frame warehouse with window guards had a coal-fed hot-air furnace to heat 27,000 square feet of space. (Author's collection.)

The large wood-frame warehouse had 90,000 square feet of space and was heated by a coal hot-air furnace. A fire destroyed one of these warehouses and its contents in 1947. It was reported that the fire was caused by the explosion of a cleaning solvent. The estimated loss from the fire was $729,889. (Author's collection.)

During the building of the barracks, tents were erected to house the troop overflow until barracks were available. One of the temporary "tar paper" buildings is on the right. In 1953, the removal of 369 tar paper–covered buildings began. (Author's collection.)

This aerial view of Fort Lawton in 1940 shows the increased number of buildings due to the World War II build-up. (Courtesy of Museum of History and Industry, Seattle, 2002.48.823.)

These soldiers are listening to war reports after the attack on Pearl Harbor on Sunday, December 7, 1941. (Author's collection.)

Thanksgiving dinner for the troops in 1942 had all the traditional trimmings. (Author's collection.)

On May 22, 1941, Fort Lawton was placed under the supervision of the commanding general of the San Francisco Port of Embarkation with the mission to support troop embarkation at Seattle. The staff of the army's 508th Port Battalion was responsible for the final processing of troops and equipment for embarkation on transport ships in Seattle's harbor. (Courtesy of Museum of History and Industry, Seattle, 1983.10.14683.5.)

The troop staging area was capable of processing a division of soldiers at one time for overseas deployment. Several port companies handled the troops and equipment, among them the 578th, 650th, and 651st. (Author's collection.)

During World War II, Fort Lawton became the second-largest port of embarkation (POE) for troops on the West Coast. Oakland, California, was the first largest. (Courtesy of National Archives and National Records Center, Seattle.)

Troops go aboard the attack transport USS *Freestone* (APA-167) sometime in 1945. The *Freestone* was built in Vancouver, Washington, and commissioned in November 1944. Between August and December 1945, the ship made two trips to the western Pacific to redeploy troops and equipment in the Philippines and various locations in Japan. On the return trips, the ship brought troops eligible for discharge back to the West Coast. The ship was decommissioned in 1946 and sold for scrap in April 1973. (Courtesy of Museum of History and Industry, Seattle, *Seattle Post-Intelligencer* collection, 1986.5.10558.1.)

Over one million troops were processed through Fort Lawton during World War II. At one time, 20,000 soldiers, the largest number during World War II, were at Fort Lawton. (Author's collection.)

A class shows soldiers how to use protective covering when under attack by enemy aircraft spraying gases. (Author's collection.)

These are instructions for soldiers learning how to operate a cargo boom for the loading and unloading of cargo aboard a ship. During World War II, numerous Engineer Corps, Quartermaster Corps, and Transportation Corps units were organized and trained at Fort Lawton. (Author's collection.)

World heavyweight boxing champion (1937–1949) Joe Louis, known as "The Brown Bomber," visited Fort Lawton and Fort Lewis during his tour of army camps during World War II. Louis, an avid horseman and horse owner, was first assigned to the cavalry when he entered the army in 1942. Louis was honorably discharged from the army in 1945. (Courtesy of National Archives, 208-FS-704-5.)

Regardless of the war, soldiers continued to play baseball, as they had in the past, on Saturdays and Sundays. Wartime duties caused some players to miss a game or two and for the same reason restricted travel to play other service teams. (Courtesy of Museum of History and Industry, Seattle, *Seattle Post-Intelligencer* collection, PI27234.)

In April 1943, the first of the Women's Army Auxiliary Corps (WAAC) arrived at Fort Lawton; their numbers increased to 200 by the end of World War II. The WAAC became the Women's Army Corps (WAC) on July 1, 1943. They operated the motor pool, worked for the POE, performed administration duties, and had a medical platoon. One of the WAC drivers was Sgt. Leah Blyth, who was assigned to drive Maj. Leon Jaworski during his temporary court-martial duty at Fort Lawton. Jaworski later became famous as the special prosecutor for the Watergate investigation during Pres. Richard M. Nixon's administration. (Courtesy of Museum of History and Industry, Seattle, 876.)

Evelyn Bender, pictured here, was one of the civilian female drivers at the Fort Lawton motor pool during World War II. Her coworkers were four American and four German POW automobile mechanics. The German prisoners of war were not allowed to drive any vehicles. "I drove," remarked Evelyn, "they did the work. I didn't even know how to drive when I got the job as a mechanics assistant. But I learned!" She learned how to be a "grease monkey" and enjoyed it. After the war, she married Geno Poalucci, one of the American mechanics she worked with. (Courtesy of Evelyn Bender Poalucci.)

Walderman Adler (right), a German POW who worked for Evelyn, returned to Germany after World War II, married, and raised a family. Adler formed a lifelong friendship with Evelyn despite the war and a non-fraternization policy. Because he was fed so well as a prisoner, Adler felt badly that his parents in Germany did not eat as well. Evelyn Bender sent a food package to his parents, and surprisingly, it was received. A Red Cross Standard Food Parcel could be mailed for $2.65. (Courtesy of Evelyn Bender Poalucci.)

Guglielmo Olivotto, born on November 23, 1911, was from Nervesa della Battaglia, Italy. Drafted into the Italian army in 1942, he was sent to Libya as a truck driver where he was captured and ultimately arrived at Fort Lawton with other Italian prisoners on May 21, 1944. About 5,000 Italian prisoners were sent to Hawaii and replaced by German prisoners. The remaining Italians at Lawton were with the Italian Service Units (ISU), which were labor units formed into three work groups—ordnance, transportation, and quartermaster functions. Their status changed from POW to ISU. (Oeste Olivotto photograph, courtesy of Dominic W. Moreo.)

Albert Marquardt was born on June 29, 1907, in Klen Sittkeim, Germany. He was 38 years old, married, and the father of two children. He was captured by American soldiers in Kaiserlauter, Germany, on March 19, 1945, and arrived at Fort Lawton in July of the same year. His death was ruled accidental by drinking poisoned alcohol. (Courtesy of Dominic W. Moreo.)

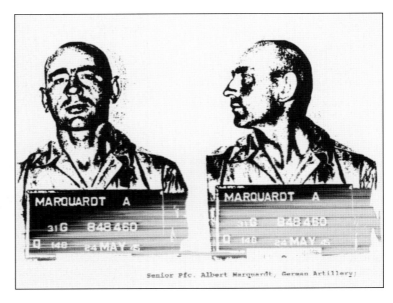

Senior Pfc. Albert Marquardt, German Artillery

The grave site of Guglielmo Olivotto at the Fort Lawton Cemetery is marked by a broken Roman column signifying a life cut short. (Author's collection.)

A small, two-pipe, bar-railing surrounding fence was erected around Olivotto's grave site sometime after 1981. (Author's collection.)

The small white fence that surrounded the grave site of Albert Marquardt in 1981 has been replaced by a concrete border. His gravestone was originally inscribed with four lines: Albert / Marquardt / German / October 1, 1945. (Author's collection.)

Sometime after 1981, a new gravestone replaced the former with six lines: a Christian cross / Albert / Marquardt / Captain / German POW / Oct 1, 1945. Marquardt's POW record listed him as a "Senior Private First Class." The change in his gravestone has not been explained. (Author's collection.)

The small shed in the background is the location of the POW grave sites. They are separated from the other grave sites at the periphery of the cemetery. (Author's collection.)

Military personnel, their families, and civilian employees of the army are buried in the four-section Fort Lawton Cemetery. The first internment was in 1902. (Author's collection.)

This parade was in observance of Fort Lawton's high ranking in the selling and purchase of war bonds during World War II. Nurses from the hospital were guests among the viewers. (Author's collection.)

German prisoners march back to their barracks after viewing film scenes of concentration camp atrocities. During World War II, 1,150 German prisoners were confined at Fort Lawton. (Courtesy of Museum of History and Industry, Seattle, *Seattle Post-Intelligencer* collection, 86.5.3533.)

On September 21, 1946, one year after the end of World War II, German prisoners were returning to Germany. Also, a group of 164 Japanese prisoners from a POW camp in Huntsville, Texas, was transited through Fort Lawton to Yokohama, Japan. (Courtesy of Museum of History and Industry, Seattle, *Seattle Post-Intelligencer* collection, PI28336.)

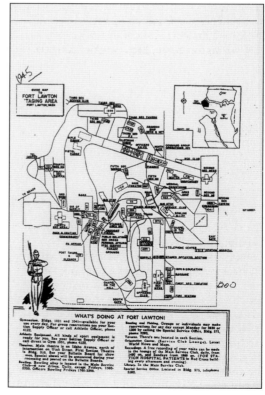

Soldiers processing through Lawton for overseas or returning had handouts showing them the staging areas and facilities available at Fort Lawton during their stay. (Author's collection.)

Because the armed forces were segregated during World War II, Service Club No. 2 at Fort Lawton was also segregated. Fort Lawton was divided into five sections or areas, and each had its own enlisted club and "tavern." Service clubs were similar to USO clubs except they were operated by the army for enlisted personnel only and were not located in the civilian community. There was no liquor served or sales of any kind permitted in the clubs. Pres. Harry S Truman desegregated the armed forces by Executive Order 9981 on July 30, 1948. (Courtesy of Black Heritage Society of Washington State, Inc., Seattle, 2004.03.207.)

Sisters Marjorie (left) and Katherine Polk were the directors of Service Club No. 2 at Fort Lawton. Service club directors worked with the army special services officer to plan and coordinate leisure-time entertainment and activities for the soldiers. The service club was a place where the soldiers could relax, read, play or listen to music, play pool, table tennis, or card games, write letters home, enjoy coffee and snacks, or just talk to the women who staffed the clubs. (Courtesy of Black Heritage Society of Washington State, Inc., Seattle, 2004.03.2.14.)

Written on the photograph, "They said it could not be done," but it was—this is the first non-segregated dance at Fort Lawton, which was held at Service Club No. 2. Soldiers are in uniform, and many of the women are wearing formal attire. One soldier is in summer uniform (khaki) and a soldier wearing the 3rd Army shoulder insignia indicates that all the soldiers were not garrisoned at Fort Lawton. (Courtesy of Black Heritage Society of Washington State, Inc., Seattle, 2004.32.29.)

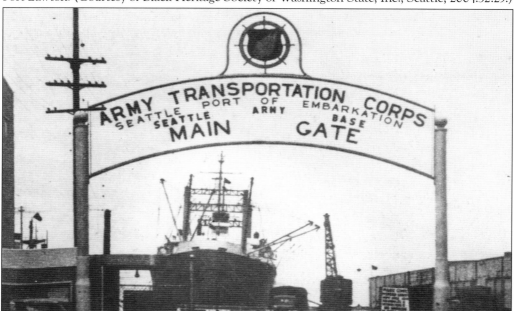

On October 1, 1949, Fort Lawton was removed from jurisdiction of the Seattle Port of Embarkation and became a separate installation. It continued to process military personnel, their dependants, and Department of Army civilian employees traveling to and from the Far East and Alaska. In July 1951, the three army division equivalents were transited to the war in Korea. Half a million personnel transited from overseas or Alaska in three years between the summer of 1951 and 1954. Seattle became the third largest POE after San Francisco and New York. (Courtesy of Ronald R. Burke.)

Benita Johnson and her daughters, three-year-old Phylis and six-month-old Becky, were among the dependants processed through Fort Lawton in March 1950. They sailed on the USNS *James O'Hara* from Seattle to Yokohama, Japan. (Courtesy of Ronald R. Burke.)

Corporals George W. Young (left) and Jack W. Jaunal transited through Fort Lawton with their unit when deployed to the war in Korea in August 1950. On his return from Korea, Young, an air gunner in the Royal Canadian Air Force during World War II, enlisted for a career in the U.S. Air Force. Jaunal, who transited through Fort Lawton as a World War II replacement, enlisted in the U.S. Marine Corps after his return from Korea. After three wars and 34 years of military service, he retired from the corps as a sergeant major. (Author's collection.)

The Korea War Memorial, located in Freedom Grove, was dedicated on Memorial Day in 1951. It is near the Blethen drinking fountain and the chapel. American casualties were 33,741 killed in action (KIA) and 103,284 wounded in action (WIA). At one time, over 8,064 were listed as missing in action (MIA). On October 12, 1998, the U.S. Congress recognized the war in Korea as officially a war under Public Law 105-261. (Author's collection.)

The Korea War Memorial is photographed here in 2007. South Korea had the largest number of KIA, with 47,000. New Zealand had the smallest number of KIA, with 31. The total number of the United Nations forces, less South Korea and the United States, was 3,170. The Korean War was second after the Civil War in the number of American casualties when compared to the actual number of troops involved. (Author's collection.)

WAC personnel (seen here in uniform) served at Fort Lawton until the 1960s, primarily as administrators. The left sleeve of the woman in the center indicates that she is a staff sergeant; two overseas bars on a sleeve indicate one year of overseas, and one service stripe, or "hash mark," indicates three years of service. The WAC on the left has a 1948–1951 gold-colored insignia of rank—an indication of a non-combat unit. The WAC on the right has a meritorious unit citation on her lower right sleeve that is no longer authorized. The Women's Army Corps was disestablished in 1978. (Author's collection.)

In the post–World War II years, one of the principal missions of Fort Lawton was to provide support for the Nike-Hercules Air Defense System operated by the 49th Air Defense Artillery Group (ADA). The control center for this system was located at Fort Lawton, consisting of a group of heavy concrete and masonry buildings and a series of specialized antenna. The 49th ADA was deactivated on May 29, 1974. (Courtesy of Museum of History and Industry, Seattle, *Seattle Post-Intelligencer* collection, 1986.5.2118.1.)

Military wives drink Coca-Cola at one of the service-club snack counters, probably during a visit to view the missile display. The *c.* 1957 menu on the wall lists a cheeseburger for 35¢. (Courtesy of Museum of History and Industry, Seattle, *Seattle Post-Intelligencer* collection, 1986.5.2120.1.)

Although the air-defense system headquarters was at Fort Lawton, the guns—90-mm anti-aircraft (AA), then the Nike-Ajax missile, followed by the Nike-Hercules missiles—were deployed on both sides of Puget Sound. The guns and missiles were never actually stationed at Fort Lawton. (Courtesy of Museum of History and Industry, Seattle, *Seattle Post-Intelligencer* collection, 1986.5.2120.2.)

A single and a double officers' family housing along Officers' Row had to be demolished in 1959 to make room for the radar site and air-defense coordinating facility. Fort Lawton was an important part of the air-defense system. Of 47 Nike units in the nation, five were in the state of Washington, and two were at Fort Lawton. (Courtesy of Museum of History and Industry, Seattle.)

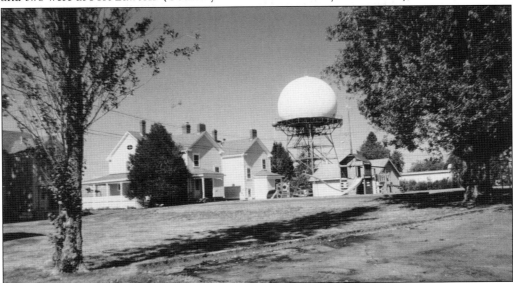

Only one of the original three radar domes, operated by the 635th Radar Squadron of the U.S. Air Force, is still in use. It is operated by the Federal Aviation Administration (FAA) as part of the national air-traffic control system. (Author's collection.)

Headquarters of the X U.S. Army Corps was located at Fort Lawton for 10 years. The X Corps was activated on May 15, 1942, at Sherman, Texas, and served in New Guinea and the Philippines during World War II. After the war, it was inactivated in Japan on January 31, 1946. Reactivated on September 15, 1950, the X Corps was assigned to the 8th U.S. Army during the Korean War and inactivated at Fort Riley, Kansas, on April 27, 1955. On January 1, 1958, the X Corps was activated again at Fort Lawton, where it remained until inactivated on March 31, 1968. (Author's collection.)

Fort Lawton administration building is seen here with the extension (left) that was added prior to World War II. It became the headquarters building for the X Corps on February 1, 1958. The army reserve and the ROTC came under the administration of the X Corps, the reserve command headquarters. When X Corps was inactivated on March 31, 1968, the 124th U.S. Army Reserve Command (ARCOM) was activated. (Author's collection.)

On July 17, 1957, ground was broken for the Harvey Hall Training Center, and it was completed in March 1958. The estimated cost of the training center, designed to accommodate 800 reservists, was $500,000. Capt. James R. Harvey, a resident of Seattle, was killed in action on June 15, 1944, while serving as a company commander in the 90th Infantry Division in Normandy, France. He was posthumously awarded the Distinguished Service Cross for his valor. (Author's collection.)

The Fort Lawton color guard stands at attention in front of a marine color guard, navy color guard, and air force color guard during a memorial service for General of the Army Douglas MacArthur on April 9, 1964, aboard the USS *Missouri*. It was aboard the *Missouri* that MacArthur accepted the formal surrender of the Japanese on September 2, 1945, V-J Day, to end World War II. (Author's collection.)

The memorial service held for General MacArthur was aboard the *Missouri*, then anchored at the navy base in Bremerton, Washington. Soldiers in the army honor guard were from Fort Lawton; to their left is the marine honor guard from the Marine Barracks, Naval Station, Bremerton. (Author's collection.)

Invited guests and other visitors sit on the port side (left) of the battleship *Missouri*, and the Bremerton High School band, navy band, and Fort Lawton honor guard observe from the starboard side (right). The USS *Missouri* was later relocated to Pearl Harbor, Hawaii. (Author's collection.)

A parade formation of X Corps soldiers is in front, and in back are Officers' Row and the radar site. Troops are in the khaki summer uniform, which is no longer issued. The army began to replace the khaki uniform in the late 1970s and 1980s. Because of manufacturing time and regulations, there is a phase-in time for a new uniform. (Author's collection.)

The largest sewage treatment plant in the Pacific Northwest, the Municipality of Metropolitan Seattle known commonly as "Metro," was dedicated July 20, 1966. The flow from the North Trunk system was diverted to the plant, eliminating the single largest raw sewage discharge in the Metro system. Fort Lawton land was leased to Seattle for 99 years but was later sold to the city. On December 31, 1995, a secondary treatment of sewage began that removed 95 percent of solids and carried out further processing until the effluent was almost clear. The upgrading of the sewage plant cost an estimated $240 million. (Courtesy of Seattle Municipal Archives, 101669.)

Units stationed at Fort Lawton in May 1973 consisted of the 124th U.S. Army Reserve Command; 6th, 89th, 222nd, 223rd, and 226th Judge Advocates detachments; 304th PIO Detachment, 50th General Hospital; 607th Medical Detachment; 1395th Army Port Detachment, 807th Signal Company; 324th Military Police Battalion; and the 341st ASA Company. An unidentified unit stands in formation in front of the enlisted barracks. (Author's collection.)

Other units stationed at Fort Lawton during the 1970s and 1980s included the U.S. Army Advisory Groups; Army Air Defense Command; 115th Military Intelligence Group; 1046th Division (Training) USAR; 49th Artillery Battalion; 124th U.S. Army Reserve Command; 365th Civil Affairs; and the U.S. Army Garrison, Fort Lawton. The theater, PX, gym, and band barracks are in the background. The WAC detachment is on the far right of the parade formation. (Author's collection.)

In front of the theater (later demolished) and other buildings, the color guard from Headquarters Company, U.S. Army Garrison, stands at the ready for a retreat ceremony at Fort Lawton on March 31, 1965. To the right of the American flag is the flag of the U.S. Army with all battle streamers. Garrison troops were permanent and provided what is known as "housekeeping," and non-garrison troops were the "renters," the non-permanent troops. (Author's collection.)

Because there were no artillery guns at Lawton, six howitzers of the 2nd Battalion, 77th Artillery, from Fort Lewis—in position on the rise from the parade ground and below the officers' quarters—fired a gun salute for one of the parades at Fort Lawton. (Author's collection.)

A retirement and retreat ceremony at Fort Lawton shows soldiers and a WAC detachment behind the color guard. The troops are wearing the summer-service khaki uniform. Only the officers were authorized to wear khaki coats; enlisted men did not. In the background to the right is the gym, and behind the trees are the enlisted barracks and theater. (Author's collection.)

On March 31, 1968, the U.S. Army X Corps was inactivated and the army designated Fort Lawton a substation of Fort Lewis. The 124th U.S. Army Reserve Command (ARCOM) was activated with its headquarters at Fort Lawton. The remaining units at Lawton included the 104th Division (Training), U.S. Army Reserve, and the U.S. Army Garrison, Fort Lawton. (Author's collection.)

Headquarters for the ARCOM was originally located in buildings erected during World War II. Three hundred and seventy World War II structures were demolished prior to the opening of Discovery Park in 1973. (Author's collection.)

The 104th Infantry Division was organized on June 21, 1921, as an army reserve division with personnel from Montana, Idaho, Wyoming, and Nevada. The division was activated for World War II at Camp Adair, Oregon, on September 15, 1942, and served in the European theater of operations. The division was inactivated on December 31, 1945, and on December 1, 1946, it was activated in Portland, Oregon, as the 104th Division (Training). The division headquarters was relocated to Vancouver, Washington, on November 1, 1961. Detachments of the 3rd and 4th Brigades were activated at Fort Lawton on January 10, 1968. In 1982, the brigades were relocated to Fort Lewis, Washington. (Author's collection.)

In March 1969, Senator Henry M. "Scoop" Jackson introduced a bill in the U.S. Senate that provided for cities to acquire federal lands at no cost for park and recreational purposes. Known as the Fort Lawton Bill, it was passed by Congress and signed by President Nixon in October 1970. Jackson served 12 years in the House of Representatives beginning on January 3, 1942, and was elected to the Senate in 1952. At the time of his death in 1983, he held the record for the longest service in Congress. Jackson was posthumously awarded the Presidential Medal of Freedom on June 26, 1984. (Courtesy of University of Washington Libraries, Special Collection, Negative UW 857.)

Plans by the Department of Defense to construct an anti–ballistic missile site at Fort Lawton in 1968 created a storm of protest by citizens of Seattle. Thanks to a Washington congressional delegation led by Sen. Warren Magnuson and Sen. Henry Jackson, and the personal intercession of Jackson with the Secretary of Defense, the plan was abandoned. On February 2, 1974, Senators Magnuson and Jackson announced that the 49th Defense Artillery Group, Army Garrison, and the Capehart housing area would be closed. The army would retain only 68 acres, which contained the reserve centers and the army cemetery. (Courtesy of University of Washington Libraries, Special Collection, Negative UW 19599.)

Beginning on March 8, 1970, about 100 Native American activists and their sympathizers laid siege to Fort Lawton outside the main gate and along the perimeter fence for 24 days. Their claim to Fort Lawton was based on treaty rights of 1865 promising reversion of surplus military lands to the original owners. At this time, the Native Americans could have requested the president of the United States to authorize, at his discretion, the issuing rations under an act of June 30, 1834, for Native Americans visiting a military post. (Courtesy of Museum of History and Industry, Seattle, *Seattle Post-Intelligencer* collection, 86.1.51939.1.)

There were three attempts by the Native Americans and their supporters to storm the gate and fence to gain entry to Lawton. Although several infiltrated into Lawton, they were removed by soldiers. Soldiers of the 3rd Armored Cavalry were sent from Fort Lewis to reinforce the military police at Fort Lawton. "Now I know how Custer felt," stated one cavalryman as about 100 Native Americans stormed the main gate. The motto of the 3rd Cavalry is, "Brave Rifles! Veterans! You have been baptized in fire and blood and have come out steel!" (Author's collection.)

Although there were confrontations between the soldiers and the Native American activists, one of their leaders, Bernie Whitebear, stated, "Our fight is not against the army but what we are trying to do is show the sincerity of our intent to gain this land." What the Native Americans failed to gain in confrontation, they achieved in the subsequent publicity that followed "the only attack by Indians on a U.S. Army fort in the Pacific Northwest in the 20th Century." Soldiers of the 104th Infantry were trained in crowd control and protest demonstrations. (Author's collection.)

Bernie Whitebear was among the Native American leaders trying to claim what was believed to be part of their historic lands. After a period of long negotiations with the City of Seattle, and Congressional intervention, an agreement was reached permitting the development of Daybreak Star Center by the United Indians of All Tribes. Bernie Whitebear directed the center for nearly 30 years before his death on July 15, 2000. (Courtesy of Museum of History and Industry, Seattle, *Seattle Post-Intelligencer* collection, 86.5.55140.)

Three

THE FINAL YEARS

Three years after he signed the Fort Lawton Bill, Pres. Richard M. Nixon, on September 1, 1972, transferred to the City of Seattle 391 acres of Fort Lawton's 1,150 acres of federal land. Acting on behalf of President Nixon, his eldest daughter, Tricia Nixon Cox, presented the deed to the mayor of Seattle in the ceremony conducted at Fort Lawton. A law signed by President Nixon on June 18, 1973, created a National Cemetery System, and 82 national cemeteries operated by the army were transferred to the Veterans Administration. Because the Fort Lawton cemetery is not a national cemetery, it is still maintained by the army. (Courtesy of National Archives, Roll-0615 Frame 02.)

On October 28, 1973, Sen. Henry Jackson dedicated Discovery Park in honor of the British sloop HMS *Discovery*, commanded by Capt. George Vancouver during the first European exploration of Puget Sound in 1792. On the platform with Jackson are former Seattle mayor Dorm Braeman, Mayor Wes Ulman, Maj. Gen. William B. Fulton, Col. Michael Citrak, Bernie Whitebear, and other civic dignitaries. (Courtesy of Seattle Municipal Archives.)

Jackson told an estimated crowd of 300 people, "The whole country owes you a debt of gratitude. You pushed me and pushed Washington. As a result of the Federal Lands for Parks and Recreation, over $100 million of surplus lands—38,000 acres—have been deeded to cities for park use." (Courtesy of Seattle Municipal Archives.)

The two bronze cannons formerly displayed at the Fort Lawton flagpole were moved to Fort Lewis prior to the transfer of land to Discovery Park. Both guns supposedly fired on commodore George Dewey's Asiatic Squadron during the Battle of Manila Bay on May 1, 1898. (Author's collection.)

The 24-pounder "Santa Caha va de Zena" was manufactured at the Manila Foundry on April 30, 1796, and bears the royal cipher of Carlos IV. The other 24-pounder, "Natividad Nuestra Senora," was also manufactured at the Manila Foundry, on September 8, 1798. (Author's collection.)

Officers' Row provided a spectacular view of the Olympic mountain range across Puget Sound. Beginning in the last half of the 18th century, the officers' quarters were located, when possible, facing the nearest large body of water, fresh or salt. (Courtesy of Library of Congress, HABS WASH, 17 SEAT, 7-3.)

The houses along Officers' Row are classic examples of 19th-century architecture designed with fine interior woodwork. They were constructed with indoor plumbing, heat provided by coal-fired furnaces, and steam radiators. Lighting was provided by kerosene or mineral oil lamps until electricity by the Seattle Electric Company was installed and completed by 1909. At this time, in 1909, the Independent Telephone Company of Seattle provided the service. (Courtesy of Library of Congress, HABS WASH, 17 SEAT, 7-L-1.)

In 1942, some of the attic rooms in the officers' quarters were modernized for a maid's room and a bath. The cost was an estimated $3,817. The original exterior color of the quarters was a dark red or "tongue," trimmed in "cedar" or brown. Later the color was white with a gray trim and roof, followed by yellow with a white trim and gray roof. During World War II, the houses were painted green. (Author's collection.)

Double NCO quarters, the first housing on the left and right, are constructed of brick; the others are wood frame. (Courtesy of Library of Congress, HABS WASH, 17-SEAT, 7-4.)

This view is from the front of the brick quarters on the right side of the street. The two brick NCO quarters were constructed in the 1930s and were the only brick buildings at Fort Lawton. They were designed on a standard plan of the Quartermaster Corps' office and are identical to some of the quarters at Fort Lewis. (Author's collection.)

This is a view of the brick NCO quarters from the back left side of the street. (Author's collection.)

This view of the double officers' quarters includes a streetlamp fixture in front of the house. The officers' quarters originally had 12 rooms, including three bathrooms, toilets, laundry, and a coal bin. (Courtesy of Library of Congress, HABS WASH, 17-SEAT, 7-K-1.)

Here are the double officers' quarters after the streetlamp fixture was removed sometime prior to 1981. (Author's collection.)

The officers' quarters had a built-in sideboard in the dining rooms. (Courtesy of Library of Congress, HABS WASH, 17-SEAT, 7-N-5.)

A brickwork basement in one of the officers' quarters shows a carpeted floor. (Courtesy of Library of Congress, HABS WASH, 17-SEAT, 7-P-3.)

Some of the officers' quarters had a tiled fireplace with an overmantel in the living room. The white oak hardwood flooring was installed in 1942. (Courtesy of Library of Congress, HABS WASH, 17-SEAT, 7-N-6.)

The brick fireplace and detailed mantel were installed in the double officers' quarters in 1937. (Courtesy of Library of Congress, HABS WASH, 17-SEAT, 7-M-3.)

Although similar in design, staircases in officers' quarters were not always identical. Some of the staircases in the officers' quarters had wood handrails in natural color or stain. (Courtesy of Library of Congress, HABS WASH, 17-SEAT, 7-X-4.)

Some of the staircases in the officers' quarters had wood handrails painted in white. Note how the stairs are not carpeted and have curved steps at floor level. (Courtesy of Library of Congress, HABS WASH, 17-SEAT, 7-N-4.)

The hospital steward's quarters was completed on April 24, 1902, at a cost of $175. It had steam heat, electric light, and water and sewer connections. The porch was enclosed in March 1912 at a cost that was more than the house, which was $246. Originally located near the hospital, it was moved to the NCO quarters area in 1938. (Courtesy of Library of Congress, HABS WASH, 17-SEAT, 7-R-1.)

The staircase in the hospital steward's quarters is painted white and of the same design as the officers' quarters. (Courtesy of Library of Congress, HABS WASH, 17-SEAT, 7-R-3.)

The double NCO quarters is viewed from a southwest direction. (Courtesy of Library of Congress, HABS WASH, 17-SEAT, 7-J-1.)

The staircase handrail in the NCO quarters is a natural color or stain. (Courtesy of Library of Congress, HABS WASH, 17-SEAT, 7-G-3.)

The band barracks were completed on March 31, 1904, at a cost of $13,314. It had a capacity for 27 band members. One room on the second floor was soundproofed with acoustical tiles. It is one of the remaining buildings in the historic district. (Courtesy of Library of Congress, HABS WASH, 17-SEAT, 7-C-1.)

The front porch of the band barracks faces the parade ground; to its left is the guardhouse, and to its right is the PX and gym. The porch has a pipe railing and Tuscan columns. (Courtesy of Library of Congress, HABS WASH, 17-SEAT, 7-C-3.)

Of the single officers' quarters, only one is left along Officers' Row. The exterior is very similar to the band barracks. (Courtesy of Library of Congress, HABS WASH, 17-SEAT, 7-X-1.)

The civilian employees' quarters was completed on February 26, 1908, at a cost of $11,645. Capacity at that time was 18 men. It had three toilets, one urinal, one bathtub, and three washbasins; six wall lockers and a shower were later installed. It was one of the first buildings that had electric lighting installed when constructed. (Courtesy of Library of Congress, HABS WASH, 17-SEAT, 7-D-1.)

This is a front view of the enlisted barracks that were completed in 1910. They were 153 feet long, 47 feet wide, and two-and-a-half-stories high and were the largest buildings at Fort Lawton. (Author's collection.)

On Saturday, February 12, 1983, one of the double enlisted barracks burned to the ground while firemen watched. It was believed the building was not saved because the City of Seattle had decided to demolish several of the structures in what is now Discovery Park. (Author's collection.)

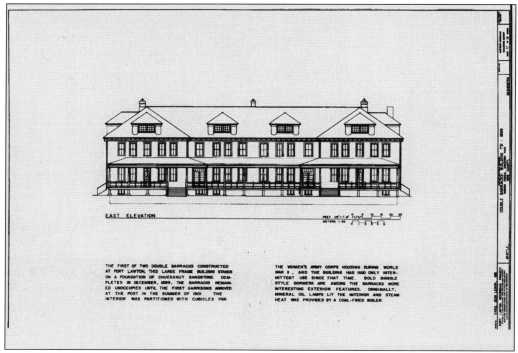

The size and measurements of the enlisted barracks is provided in this drawing. (Courtesy of Library of Congress, Historic American Buildings Survey, "Fort Lawton: A Record.")

The enlisted quarters, viewed from the rear, were completed in 1910, and the last were demolished in 1980s. (Courtesy of Library of Congress, HABS WASH, 17-SEAT, 1-F-3.)

The guardhouse is the only nonresident building that was always used for its original purpose. It was later designated as a MP station until 1975, when it was re-designated as a security guard station. (Courtesy of Library of Congress, HABS WASH, 17-SEAT, 7-Q-1.)

The guardhouse had a capacity for 25 prisoners held in two steel cages and three solitary cells. The original cost for the confinement cells was $315. On February 22, 1922, one soldier from the 58th Infantry awaiting sentence for theft and one soldier from the 21st Infantry awaiting sentence for desertion were found on the floor of their cell unconscious from an overdose of morphine, supposedly smuggled into the guardhouse. (Courtesy of Library of Congress, HABS WASH, 17-SEAT, 7-Q-3.)

The bake house was completed on April 24, 1902, at a cost of $1,870. Mineral oil was used for lighting, and electricity was installed in 1905. The entry was reconstructed in 1940, ovens were removed, and the interior remodeled as office space during World War II. (Courtesy of Library of Congress, HABS WASH, 17-SEAT, 7-B-1.)

The removal of the chapel from what is now Discovery Park has been suggested. Because of protests by some concerned citizens and groups, the chapel remains. Constructed in 1942, it is the last World War II building in the park. (Author's collection.)

The hospital, completed in 1900, was highly recommended for retention because of its historical significance and probable interest to Discovery Park visitors. Although the building had been modernized for use as an office building, much of the interior detailing had been maintained in its historic character. Although recommended for retention, it was demolished. (Author's collection.)

The post-exchange, or PX, was completed on May 2, 1905, at a cost of $20,710. The building was equipped with a gymnasium, pool tables, a reading room, and a lunch counter. On June 11, 1939, an addition was built for use as a "beer parlor" at a cost of $7,191. (Author's collection.)

The last of the original bus stops was built during the World War II era and was painted white with a gray painted bench. (1981). (Author's collection.)

The restored bus stop was painted yellow, including the bench, in 2007. (Author's collection.)

The quartermaster stable was completed on April 24, 1902, at a cost of $2,941. It consisted of 36 animal stalls, a wagon room, harness room, grain room, and a loft. In 1940, it was converted to a warehouse. (Courtesy of Library of Congress, HABS WASH, 17-SEAT, 7-V-1.)

The quartermaster warehouse and office are among the buildings that have been demolished. (Courtesy of Library of Congress, HABS WASH, 17-SEAT, 7-Y-1.)

A general view of Fort Lawton shows the guardhouse on the extreme left, quartermaster storehouse and office in the center background, bus stop shelter at center front, and to the extreme right the warehouse and stable. (Courtesy of Library of Congress, HABS WASH, 17-SEAT, 7-1.)

The administration building was completed on April 24, 1902, at a cost of $4,007, with wood-frame walls and floors, a brick foundation, and sewer and water connections. Electric lights were installed on March 1, 1907, and a hot water heating system the same year. A fire-siren motor, a fire gong, and a code machine were installed in 1937. In 1939, a fire-alarm system was installed and a drinking fountain six months later. A hot water tank was installed in 1940. (Courtesy of National Archives, Record Group 77.)

The administration building is seen here before the World War II extension and back porch area was removed. The building is one of the original structures in Colonial Revival style and is placed for a commanding view of Puget Sound, the Olympic Mountains, and the parade ground. (Courtesy of Library of Congress, HABS WASH, 17-SEAT, 7-A-1.)

The administration building is now maintained by Discovery Park. The World War II extension and back porch have been removed. (Author's collection.)

The 70th Regional Readiness Command (RRC) is one of 10 major subordinate commands of the army reserve. The 70th RRC is responsible for Oregon, Washington, and Idaho. Prior to 2003, all Regional Readiness Commands were designated Regional Support Commands. The mission of the RRC is to provide trained and ready soldiers and units capable of rapid mobilization if activated. (Author's collection.)

The 124th U.S. Army Reserve Command (ARCOM) was a pre-mobilization command of army reserve units in Washington, Oregon, Northern California, and northwestern Nevada. ARCOM was responsible for manning, training, and equipping its subordinate units to enable them to perform their mobilization missions. Upon mobilization, these subordinate units would be reassigned to support an active army command. The 124th ARCOM was inactivated in 1996 and became the 70th Regional Support Command. (Author's collection.)

The Trailblazer Memorial was dedicated to the 70th Infantry Division on June 25, 2000, by the 70th Regional Support Command of the U.S. Army. The form of the monument is a replica of the memorial erected by the District of Forback in France on Spicheren Heights on the 50th anniversary of V-E Day, May 8, 1945. (Author's collection.)

The 70th Infantry Division arrived in France in December 1944 during the Battle of the Ardennes. Assigned to the 3rd Army, commanded by Gen. George S. Patton, the division was in Germany when the war in Europe ended. (Author's collection.)

The smokestack was originally part of the Fort Lawton laundry before the laundry building was demolished. Because the smokestack was more expensive to take down than to leave standing, it remains. Later the 70th Division insignia was painted on it. An old local legend is that the stack was part of a crematorium because so many horses and mules arrived on post but were never seen again. In reality, the animals were shipped to the Philippines and did not come out again. (Author's collection.)

On September 23, 1972, the U.S. Army Reserve Center was dedicated in honor of 2nd Lt. Robert R. Leisy. Leisy was awarded the Medal of Honor for his extraordinary courage against the enemy in Phuoc Long Province, Vietnam. He was killed on December 2, 1969, while serving with Company B, 1st Battalion, 8th Cavalry Regiment, 1st Cavalry Division. (Author's collection.)

At the top of the stairs is the Army Reserve Center, which is known by its acronym FLARC. It has never received a name like the other reserve centers or given a dedication; it is only known as FLARC, or the Fort Lawton Army Reserve Center. (Author's collection.)

FLARC was constructed at a cost of $14 million to replace the old World War II wooden building. Because Fort Lawton is scheduled to be closed in 2009, the reserve command will be moved and reserve training will be conducted at Fort Lewis. (Author's collection.)

A brick pyramid monument is crowned by a light, with the words, "Iraq 2003 NEVER FORGET in Honor of Fallen Soldiers." (Author's collection.)

On November 14, 1957, the Capehart housing at Lawton was dedicated Buckey Heights in honor of 1st Lt. Mervyn C. Buckey, the first commander of Fort Lawton. It was the first military housing at Fort Lawton since 1943. Buckey Heights contained 66 housing units, 44 for enlisted and 22 for officers. In September 2007, the City of Seattle agreed to purchase the Capehart housing area from the federal government for $11.1 million. The removal of the Capehart housing in the agreement will restore 24 acres of land to Discovery Park. (Author's collection.)

On September 27, 1975, ground-breaking for Daybreak Star took place, and in 1977, the Daybreak Star Indian Culture Center was completed. The center is operated by the United Indians of All Tribes Foundation, a private, nonprofit corporation that was founded in Seattle, Washington, in 1970. (Author's collection.)

Discovery Park is fortunate to have several of Fort Lawton's original buildings still intact and echoing the tradition of its military heritage. It is important to remember that once a historic building or structure has been destroyed, it is not only impossible to resurrect it in detail, but it would also be financially prohibitive. The original administration building and the flagpole with its flag are symbolic of that military heritage. (Author's collection.)

At the base of the flagpole is a plaque dedicated to Henry M. Jackson: "This viewpoint is dedicated by a grateful city to the memory of Henry M. Jackson. It was through his efforts and vision as United States Senator that this magnificent park became a reality. Because of him, surplus federal lands were used to create not only this great park, but countless other parks throughout the land. The vista which spreads before you is symbolic of the vision which brought this park into being. 1984." (Author's collection.)

The flagpole at the Henry M. Jackson viewpoint was erected in 1946 and is located in front of and halfway between the administration building and Officers' Row. The plaque dedicated to Senator Jackson was placed at the base in 1984. (Author's collection.)

ACROSS AMERICA, PEOPLE ARE DISCOVERING SOMETHING WONDERFUL. *THEIR HERITAGE.*

Arcadia Publishing is the leading local history publisher in the United States. With more than 4,000 titles in print and hundreds of new titles released every year, Arcadia has extensive specialized experience chronicling the history of communities and celebrating America's hidden stories, bringing to life the people, places, and events from the past. To discover the history of other communities across the nation, please visit:

www.arcadiapublishing.com

Customized search tools allow you to find regional history books about the town where you grew up, the cities where your friends and family live, the town where your parents met, or even that retirement spot you've been dreaming about.